The

Cookbook

SMITHMARK

Contents

Introduction

The Sweet 'N Low Cookbook features delicious recipes that focus on good health and nutrition. Too much sugar, fat, and sodium in your diet may contribute to cavities, obesity, heart disease, hypertension, and other health problems.

Sweet 'N Low, Butter Buds, and Nu-Salt provide a tasty alternative to sugar, butter, oil, and salt.

The recipes included here are not only good for you and easy to make, they taste good too! All the recipes have been tested, and the fat, sugar, and salt contents have been reduced to conform to the U.S. Dietary Guideline recommendations. Each recipe lists the number of calories per serving, as well as the carbohydrate, protein, fat, sodium, and cholesterol content in each serving. The recipes recommend that you use a nonstick pan to prepare your meal; if a nonstick pan is not available, you may spray your pan with a nonstick coating agent instead.

The recipes in this book prove that low-calorie, nutritious meals don't have to be bland, boring, or tasteless. By following these recipes, you'll find that you can keep on a diet while still looking forward to every meal!

Appetizers and Soups

Stuffed Cabbage *18 servings*

2 medium-size onions, cut in chunks
1 large head cabbage
2 pounds lean ground veal or beef
Freshly ground pepper to taste

1 teaspoon garlic powder
2 cups tomato juice, divided
4 packets Sweet 'N Low®
2 tablespoons lemon juice

In large saucepan, cook onions and cabbage in boiling water about 5 minutes. Drain, leaving onions in saucepan and removing cabbage. Mix ground meat with pepper, garlic powder, and ½ cup tomato juice. Divide in 18 portions. Separate cabbage leaves and place a portion of meat on each. Roll up and fasten with toothpick. Place in saucepan with onions. Stir Sweet 'N Low and lemon juice into remaining tomato juice. Pour over all. Cover and gently simmer 1 hour, or until cabbage is tender and meat is cooked through.

PER SERVING (1 cabbage roll):		Calories: 96	Cholesterol: 41mg
Protein: 11gm	Carbohydrate: 5gm	Fat: 4gm	Sodium: 151mg

Barbecued Spareribs *24 servings*

2 pounds pork spareribs
1 cup apple juice
1 tablespoon soy sauce

2 tablespoons hoisin sauce or catsup
1 tablespoon honey
1 packet Sweet 'N Low

In saucepan of boiling water, simmer ribs about 5 minutes to remove excess fat. Drain. In shallow baking dish, combine remaining ingredients. Add ribs and marinate 2 to 3 hours. Preheat oven to 350°F. Bake, uncovered, 45 minutes. Increase temperature to 450°F and continue baking 5 to 10 minutes, or until very tender.

PER SERVING (1 rib):		Calories: 68	Cholesterol: 18mg
Protein: 4gm	Carbohydrate: 2gm	Fat: 4gm	Sodium: 100mg

Paprika Meatballs   *16 meatballs*

1 pound lean ground beef
⅓ cup liquid Butter Buds®
3 tablespoons minced onion
2 tablespoons fine bread crumbs
¼ teaspoon garlic powder
⅛ teaspoon dry mustard
⅛ teaspoon pepper

1 medium-size ripe tomato, chopped
½ teaspoon basil
¼ teaspoon thyme
2 cups low fat milk, divided
1 packet Butter Buds
3 tablespoons all-purpose flour
2 teaspoons paprika

In large bowl, combine beef, Butter Buds, onion, bread crumbs, garlic powder, mustard, and pepper and mix thoroughly. Shape mixture into 16 cocktail-size meatballs. Brown in large nonstick skillet over medium heat about 10 to 15 minutes, or until meatballs are browned on all sides. Remove from skillet and drain off excess fat. Combine tomato, basil, and thyme in same skillet. Cook until tomato is very soft, about 5 to 10 minutes. In saucepan, heat 1½ cups milk until warm. Add Butter Buds and stir until dissolved. Add flour and paprika to remaining milk and stir to a smooth paste. Add to heated milk mixture and blend thoroughly. Slowly add cooked tomato to milk mixture, stirring constantly. Transfer mixture to large skillet and add meatballs. Heat thoroughly just until hot. Do not boil.

PER SERVING (1 meatball):   Calories: 86   Cholesterol: 19mg
Protein: 7gm   Carbohydrate: 5gm   Fat: 4gm   Sodium: 108mg

By using Butter Buds instead of butter in this recipe, you have saved 80 calories and 30 mg cholesterol per serving.

Mock Herring   *About 3 cups*

2 medium onions, sliced
2 stalks celery, cut into 1-inch pieces
1 small eggplant, peeled and cut into
   long strips, 1-inch wide
1 cup plain low fat yogurt

1 tablespoon lemon juice
1 packet Sweet 'N Low
¼ teaspoon salt
⅛ teaspoon ground cloves
1 bay leaf

Steam onions and celery in vegetable steamer over boiling water 5 to 6 minutes. Add eggplant and steam about 5 minutes, or until soft but not mushy. Remove vegetables to bowl and set aside to cool. In separate bowl, combine remaining ingredients; mix gently with cooled vegetables. Remove bay leaf. Chill thoroughly. Serve on whole-grain bread or crackers.

PER SERVING (⅓ cup):   Calories: 47   Cholesterol: 2mg
Protein: 3gm   Carbohydrate: 8gm   Fat: 1gm   Sodium: 132mg

Paprika Meatballs, Cheesy Fish Chowder (page 14),
Herb Salad Dressing (page 42)

De-Lish Fish Soup *6 servings*

4 cups water
¾ teaspoon salt
1 bay leaf
2 pounds fresh fish fillets (sole or
    flounder)
1 cup thinly sliced celery
1 cup thinly sliced carrots

1 can (1 pound) tomatoes
1 cup peeled, diced potatoes
4 thinly sliced green onions
2 teaspoons dillweed
2 packets Sweet 'N Low
Freshly ground pepper to taste

In large saucepan, bring water to a boil. Add salt, bay leaf, and fish. Gently simmer, uncovered, 10 minutes. Remove fish and set aside. Strain broth and bring to boil again. Add celery, carrots, tomatoes, and potatoes. Cover and simmer 10 minutes, or until vegetables are tender. Flake fish and add to saucepan, with green onions, dillweed, and Sweet 'N Low. Allow to heat through without boiling. Season with pepper.

PER SERVING (1 cup):   Calories: 189   Cholesterol: 73mg
Protein: 30gm   Carbohydrate: 11gm   Fat: 1gm   Sodium: 548mg

Cheesy Fish Chowder *5 servings*

3 medium-size (about 1 pound) whole
    potatoes, peeled and cut up
⅔ cup chopped onions
½ cup water
1 packet Butter Buds, *made into liquid*
¼ teaspoon freshly ground pepper

¼ teaspoon paprika
3 cups low fat milk
4 ounces reduced-fat cheese food, cut up
1 pound cod or flounder fillets, cut into
    small pieces
1½ tablespoons chopped fresh parsley

In large saucepan, combine potatoes, onions, water, Butter Buds, pepper, and paprika. Bring to a boil. Reduce heat and simmer 15 minutes, or until potatoes are tender; do not drain. In separate saucepan, heat milk with cheese over low heat about 10 minutes, stirring constantly until cheese has melted. Do not boil. Add fish to potato mixture and cook until tender, about 3 minutes. Stir hot cheese mixture into soup; heat just until hot. Sprinkle with parsley before serving. (See photo, page 13.)

PER SERVING (1¼ cups):   Calories: 264   Cholesterol: 57mg
Protein: 27gm   Carbohydrate: 24gm   Fat: 6gm   Sodium: 592mg

By using Butter Buds instead of butter in this recipe, you have saved 150 calories and 56 mg cholesterol per serving.

Asparagus Soup   *4 servings*

1 can (16 ounces) cut asparagus,
  undrained
1 chicken-flavor bouillon cube
1 cup water
2 tablespoons minced onion flakes

¹/₂ cup evaporated skim milk, undiluted
2 tablespoons chopped fresh parsley
1 packet Sweet 'N Low
Freshly ground pepper to taste

In medium-size saucepan, combine asparagus with liquid, bouillon, water, and onion flakes. Simmer about 5 minutes. Stir in remaining ingredients. Heat but do not boil.

PER SERVING (¾ cup):   Calories: 50   Cholesterol: 1mg
Protein: 5gm   Carbohydrate: 8gm   Fat: trace   Sodium: 710mg

Borscht   *2 servings*

1 can (8 ounces) beets, undrained
¹/₂ cup plain low fat yogurt

1 tablespoon lemon juice
1 packet Sweet 'N Low

Place all ingredients in blender container. Cover and process at low speed 5 to 10 seconds. Mixture should be chunky. Chill.

PER SERVING (1 cup):   Calories: 72   Cholesterol: 3mg
Protein: 4gm   Carbohydrate: 13gm   Fat: trace   Sodium: 341mg

Cream of Tomato Soup   *6 servings*

1 cup instant nonfat dry milk
1 can (46 fluid ounces) tomato juice,
  divided
2 tablespoons minced onion flakes
2 tablespoons chopped fresh parsley
2 teaspoons distilled white vinegar

¹/₂ teaspoon basil
¹/₂ teaspoon salt
1 bay leaf
2 whole cloves
1 packet Sweet 'N Low

Place milk powder in bowl. Gradually add 1½ cups tomato juice, stirring to form a smooth paste. Set aside. In large saucepan, combine remaining tomato juice and other ingredients, except Sweet 'N Low, and simmer about 5 minutes. Remove bay leaf and cloves. Pour some of the hot liquid into the tomato-milk paste; stir, then pour mixture back into saucepan. Heat slowly, stirring constantly, to serving temperature. Do not boil. Stir in Sweet 'N Low.

PER SERVING (1 cup):   Calories: 86   Cholesterol: 2mg
Protein: 6gm   Carbohydrate: 17gm   Fat: trace   Sodium: 1090mg

Salads

Yogurt Fruit Salad *6 servings*

*1 container (8 ounces) plain low fat
  yogurt*
3 packets Sweet 'N Low
1 tablespoon lemon juice
3 oranges, peeled and sectioned

*1 medium-size Red Delicious apple,
  diced*
*2 medium-size bananas, peeled and
  sliced*
½ cup chopped pecans

In large bowl, combine yogurt, Sweet 'N Low, and lemon juice. Add fruit and pecans, tossing to coat thoroughly. Chill.

PER SERVING (¾ cup):	Calories: 173		Cholesterol: 2mg
Protein: 4gm	Carbohydrate: 27gm	Fat: 7gm	Sodium: 29mg

Grated Carrot Condiment *8 servings*

*4¼ cups coarsely grated carrots (about
  1¼ pounds)*
½ teaspoon Nu-Salt® salt substitute
¼ cup red wine vinegar

*1 tablespoon finely chopped fresh
  jalapeño peppers*
¼ cup raisins
¼ teaspoon Sweet 'N Low

In large bowl, stir together carrots and Nu-Salt; let stand at room temperature about 30 minutes. Place carrots between paper towels and squeeze to absorb excess moisture. In another large bowl, combine vinegar, jalapeño peppers, raisins, and Sweet 'N Low; stir until Sweet 'N Low dissolves. Stir in carrots until well blended. Let mixture marinate at room temperature at least 15 minutes before serving.

PER SERVING (½ cup)	Calories: 40		Cholesterol: 0mg
Protein: 1gm	Carbohydrate: 10gm	Fat: 0gm	Sodium: 37mg

Grated Carrot Condiment

Cottage Tuna Salad   *4 servings*

*1 can (6½ ounces) tuna, packed in
   water, drained*
1 cup low fat cottage cheese
¼ cup chopped celery
¼ cup chopped green onion
2 tablespoons chopped fresh parsley
1 tablespoon capers

¼ cup plain low fat yogurt
1 tablespoon lemon juice
½ teaspoon dry mustard
1 packet Sweet 'N Low
¼ teaspoon freshly ground pepper
¼ teaspoon salt

In medium bowl, combine tuna, cottage cheese, celery, green onion, parsley, and capers. Mix remaining ingredients in separate bowl. Add to tuna mixture and mix thoroughly. Cover and chill.

PER SERVING (½ cup):   Calories: 110   Cholesterol: 20mg
Protein: 20gm   Carbohydrate: 4gm   Fat: 1gm   Sodium: 585mg

Christmas Eve Salad   *8 servings*

1 can (8¼ ounces) sliced beets
*1 can (8 ounces) chunk pineapple,
   packed in juice*
1 medium orange, pared and sectioned
1 pink grapefruit, pared and sectioned
2 bananas, sliced
*½ jicama, pared and sliced, or 1 can (8
   ounces) water chestnuts, drained and
   sliced*

2 tablespoons lemon juice
1 teaspoon Sweet 'N Low, divided
3 cups shredded lettuce
1 lime, cut into wedges
¼ cup blanched almond slivers
1 tablespoon anise seed

Drain beets and pineapple, reserving liquid. In large bowl, combine beets, pineapple, orange, grapefruit, bananas, and jicama (or water chestnuts). In small bowl, combine reserved beet and pineapple liquids, lemon juice, and ½ teaspoon Sweet 'N Low. Pour over fruit. Let stand 10 minutes; drain. In serving bowl, arrange fruit on shredded lettuce. Garnish with lime wedges and almonds. In cup, combine anise seed and remaining ½ teaspoon Sweet 'N Low; sprinkle over salad.

PER SERVING (about 1 cup):   Calories: 115   Cholesterol: 0mg
Protein: 2gm   Carbohydrate: 24gm   Fat: 2gm   Sodium: 85mg

Main Dishes
Beef

Teriyaki Beef Kabobs *4 servings*

1 packet Butter Buds, *made into liquid*
2 tablespoons dry sherry
1 tablespoon lemon juice
1 tablespoon soy sauce
2 teaspoons sugar
1 clove garlic, minced
¼ teaspoon ginger

1 pound top round beef, cut into
  1½-inch chunks
1 medium-size green pepper, seeded and
  cut into 1-inch chunks
1 can (8 ounces) juice-packed pineapple
  chunks, drained
1 medium-size onion, cut into 1-inch
  chunks

In medium-size bowl, combine Butter Buds, sherry, lemon juice, soy sauce, sugar, garlic, and ginger. Add beef and stir to coat thoroughly. Cover and refrigerate 2 to 3 hours, stirring occasionally. Remove beef cubes and reserve marinade. Thread beef, green pepper, pineapple, and onion alternately on four 10-inch wood or metal skewers. Cook 10 to 15 minutes on preheated barbecue grill, turning once during cooking and basting several times with marinade.

PER SERVING (1 skewer):		Calories: 228		Cholesterol: 65mg
Protein: 27gm	Carbohydrate: 17gm		Fat: 5gm	Sodium: 490mg

By using Butter Buds instead of vegetable oil in this recipe, you have saved 228 calories per serving.
Nice to know: *One packet of Sweet 'N Low will work just as well in this recipe as 2 teaspoons sugar. You'll save 5 calories and 2 gm carbohydrate per serving.*

Marinated Pork Chops (page 24), Teriyaki Beef Kabobs

Chili Con Carne *10 servings*

1⅓ cups (about 8 ounces) dried kidney beans
5 cups water, divided
1 bay leaf
1 dried chili pepper
1½ pounds lean ground beef
½ cup (1 medium-size) chopped onion
½ cup (1 small) chopped green pepper
1 large clove garlic, minced
⅛ teaspoon cayenne
½ teaspoon oregano
1 teaspoon cumin
¼ cup chopped fresh parsley
1 packet Butter Buds
2 pounds (about 6 medium-size) ripe tomatoes, chopped
1 can (6 ounces) salt-free tomato paste

Wash kidney beans and remove blemished ones. Place in large saucepan with 4 cups water, bay leaf, and chili pepper. Boil 2 minutes; reduce heat to simmering. Cover and simmer until beans are tender, about 2 hours. Remove bay leaf. Brown beef, onion, and green pepper in large skillet. Drain excess fat. Add to cooked beans. Add garlic, cayenne, oregano, cumin, parsley, Butter Buds, tomatoes, tomato paste, and remaining 1 cup water to bean mixture. Cover and simmer 1 hour, stirring occasionally.

PER SERVING (1 cup): Calories: 299 Cholesterol: 51mg
Protein: 19gm Carbohydrate: 23gm Fat: 15gm Sodium: 140mg

By using Butter Buds instead of vegetable oil in this recipe, you have saved 90 calories per serving.

Hungarian Goulash *6 servings*

1½ pounds cubed lean beef
2 medium onions, sliced
1 can (1 pound) whole tomatoes
1 can (8 ounces) tomato sauce
1½ tablespoons paprika
1 packet Sweet 'N Low
Freshly ground pepper to taste
3 cups cooked (6 ounces uncooked) whole-wheat or spinach noodles
1 cup plain low fat yogurt

In medium-size nonstick saucepan, brown beef on all sides. Remove beef and set aside. In same saucepan, cook onions until transparent. Return beef to pan and add tomatoes, tomato sauce, paprika, Sweet 'N Low, and pepper. Cover and simmer over very low heat 1 hour. Uncover slightly and let simmer 30 minutes, or until meat is tender and sauce has reduced a little. Meanwhile, prepare noodles according to package directions, omitting salt. Remove goulash from heat. Stir in yogurt. Reheat to serving temperature without boiling. Serve over hot noodles.

PER SERVING (1¼ cups): Calories: 323 Cholesterol: 68mg
Protein: 34gm Carbohydrate: 31gm Fat: 7gm Sodium: 444mg

Pork, Veal, and Lamb

Stuffed Breast of Veal *12 servings*

Stuffing
3 tablespoons liquid Butter Buds
1 medium onion, chopped
3 cloves garlic, minced
¼ pound ground veal
¼ pound fresh spinach, finely chopped
2 egg whites
1 egg yolk
½ cup chopped parsley
⅓ cup uncooked wild rice
¼ cup brandy
1 teaspoon Nu-Salt *salt substitute*
½ teaspoon freshly ground pepper

Veal Breast
¼ teaspoon Nu-Salt *salt substitute,*
   divided
¼ teaspoon freshly ground pepper,
   divided
1 veal breast, with pocket for stuffing
   (4¾-5 pounds), boned
2 tablespoons vegetable oil
2 teaspoons dry Butter Buds
2 cloves garlic, minced
1 bay leaf
2 envelopes low-sodium instant chicken
   broth and seasoning mix, made into
   liquid (1½ cups)
¾ cup sweet vermouth
⅛ teaspoon Sweet 'N Low
1 medium carrot, sliced
1 medium onion, sliced

In small nonstick skillet over medium heat, heat liquid Butter Buds. Add chopped onion and 3 cloves garlic and cook until slightly tender. Remove to large bowl; stir in remaining stuffing ingredients. Preheat oven to 350°F. Sprinkle ⅛ teaspoon Nu-Salt and ⅛ teaspoon pepper into pocket of veal breast. Fill loosely with stuffing; do not overfill. Seal opening of pocket by pressing edges together. Sprinkle remaining ⅛ teaspoon each Nu-Salt and pepper onto exterior of meat. In large flameproof casserole or roasting pan over medium heat, heat oil. Add veal and brown on all sides. Add remaining ingredients; bring to a boil. Bake, covered, about 1½ hours. Uncover and bake, basting occasionally with pan juices, about 30 minutes. Remove meat to platter and keep warm. Skim fat from pan juices and remove bay leaf. Over high heat, cook, stirring, until thickened and reduced to 1 cup. Cut veal into 12 slices and serve with sauce. (See photo, page 25.)

PER SERVING (1 slice):   Calories: 355   Cholesterol: 128mg
Protein: 29gm   Carbohydrate: 5gm   Fat: 24gm   Sodium: 102mg

Marinated Pork Chops   *4 servings*

1 packet Butter Buds, *mixed with ¼ cup hot water*
¼ cup red wine
3 tablespoons chopped onion
2 teaspoons freshly squeezed lemon juice with pulp
1 bay leaf

1 large clove garlic, crushed
¼ teaspoon crushed rosemary
¼ teaspoon thyme
¼ teaspoon dry mustard
⅛ teaspoon freshly ground pepper
4 pork chops (about 1½ pounds)

Combine all ingredients except pork chops and blend thoroughly. Pour into large, shallow glass bowl. Marinate pork chops, completely covered, 4 to 6 hours or overnight. Preheat oven to 350°F. Remove chops from marinade and bake in square baking dish 20 to 25 minutes or cook outdoors on charcoal grill.
(See photo, page 21.)

PER SERVING (1 pork chop):		Calories: 202	Cholesterol: 73mg
Protein: 26gm	Carbohydrate: 4gm	Fat: 8gm	Sodium: 247mg

By using Butter Buds instead of vegetable oil in this recipe, you have saved 228 calories per serving.

Lamb Curry   *4 servings*

1 medium-size onion, diced
1 tablespoon vegetable oil
1½ pounds lean lamb, cubed
2 tablespoons all-purpose flour
1 or 2 teaspoons curry powder
¼ teaspoon ginger

1 medium-size apple, peeled and diced
1 cup beef-flavored bouillon
2 tablespoons raisins
1 tablespoon chutney
1 packet Sweet 'N Low
½ cup plain low fat yogurt

In medium saucepan, sauté onion in vegetable oil. Dredge lamb cubes in flour. Add to saucepan and cook 3 to 4 minutes, or until lightly browned. Add curry powder and ginger. Stir and continue cooking 1 minute. Add apple, bouillon, raisins, and chutney. Cover and simmer gently 1½ hours, or until very tender. Add ¼ cup water if necessary. Stir in Sweet 'N Low and yogurt. Serve over hot cooked rice with assorted condiments, such as chopped raw vegetables and fruits (green pepper, cucumber, tomato, banana, or raisins).

PER SERVING (1 cup):		Calories: 348	Cholesterol: 112mg
Protein: 37gm	Carbohydrate: 19gm	Fat: 13gm	Sodium: 480mg

Stuffed Breast of Veal (page 23)

Chicken

Chicken Couscous   *8 servings*

Chicken

2 tablespoons olive oil
1 broiler-fryer chicken (2½-3 pounds),
    cut up and skin removed
4 small carrots, cut into pieces
    1" × 2½"
2 medium onions, sliced
1 pound turnips, peeled and diced
    (about 3 cups)
2 cloves garlic, finely minced
2½ teaspoons ground coriander
1 teaspoon low-sodium instant chicken
    broth and seasoning mix
½ teaspoon Nu-Salt *salt substitute*
½ teaspoon ground turmeric

¼ teaspoon cayenne pepper
1 cup water
¼ cup dry white wine
3 zucchini, peeled and cut into ¼-inch
    slices (about 6 cups)
1 can (1 pound) chick-peas, drained

Couscous

1⅓ cups couscous
⅓ cup currants
¼ teaspoon Nu-Salt *salt substitute*
1⅓ cups boiling water
2 tablespoons margarine
½ cup liquid Butter Buds
1 teaspoon ground turmeric

In Dutch oven over medium-high heat, heat oil. Add chicken and cook 15 minutes or until brown on all sides. Remove chicken to platter. Drain fat from Dutch oven and add carrots, onions, turnips, garlic, coriander, broth mix, Nu-Salt, turmeric, and cayenne. Pour water and wine over vegetables. Bring to a boil. Reduce heat to low; simmer, covered, stirring occasionally, about 10 minutes. Return chicken to Dutch oven; simmer, covered, about 20 minutes. Add zucchini and simmer, covered, 10 minutes or until thickest pieces of chicken are done and vegetables are tender. Add chick-peas and simmer about 5 minutes.

Prepare couscous: In large bowl, combine couscous, currants, and Nu-Salt; stir in boiling water. Let stand 2 to 3 minutes or until water is absorbed. In large nonstick skillet over medium heat, melt margarine. Add Butter Buds, couscous, and turmeric; cook, stirring, about 4 minutes.

Mound couscous on heated platter; arrange chicken and vegetables around couscous. In Dutch oven over high heat, reduce pan juices to 1 cup. Serve separately.

PER SERVING (1 piece of chicken, 1 cup vegetables, ½ cup couscous):

	Calories: 325		Cholesterol: 72mg
Protein: 34gm	Carbohydrate: 40gm	Fat: 6gm	Sodium: 425mg

Chicken Couscous

Coq Au Vin *4 servings*

*2¹/₂-pound broiler-fryer, cut up and
  skinned*
1¹/₄ cups tomato juice
¹/₄ cup red wine vinegar
1 chicken-flavor bouillon cube, crushed
1 clove garlic, crushed
1 packet Sweet 'N Low

1¹/₂ cups small whole onions, peeled
*2 cups (about 4 ounces) quartered fresh
  mushrooms*
1 sprig parsley
1 bay leaf
1 teaspoon marjoram
1 teaspoon sage
1 teaspoon rosemary

Place chicken pieces in shallow baking dish. In separate bowl, combine tomato juice, vinegar, bouillon, garlic, and Sweet 'N Low. Pour over chicken. Allow to marinate, refrigerated, 3 to 4 hours. Remove chicken and reserve marinade in small bowl. Preheat oven to 375°F. Brown chicken and onions in nonstick skillet. Return to baking dish. Add mushrooms. Tie herbs in cheesecloth and add to chicken. Pour marinade over all. Cover and bake 30 to 35 minutes. Baste with marinade sauce and continue baking, uncovered, 15 to 20 minutes, or until chicken is tender. Remove herbs before serving.

PER SERVING (¼ chicken):   Calories: 212   Cholesterol: 95mg
Protein: 32gm   Carbohydrate: 11gm   Fat: 5gm   Sodium: 660mg

Orange Herbed Chicken *4 servings*

*2¹/₂-pound chicken, quartered and
  skinned*
1 packet Butter Buds, *made into liquid*
*¹/₄ cup frozen orange juice concentrate,
  undiluted*

2 packets Sweet 'N Low
1 teaspoon oregano
1 teaspoon dry mustard

Place chicken in large skillet. In separate bowl, combine remaining ingredients and pour over chicken. Cover and simmer gently 20 minutes. Turn chicken and baste with sauce. Cover and simmer 15 to 20 minutes, or until chicken is tender. Transfer chicken to serving platter and pour sauce over chicken.

PER SERVING (¼ chicken):   Calories: 208   Cholesterol: 96mg
Protein: 30gm   Carbohydrate: 10gm   Fat: 4gm   Sodium: 278mg

By using Butter Buds instead of butter in this recipe, you have saved 188 calories and 70 mg cholesterol per serving.

Fish and Seafood

Ginger Teriyaki Fish   *6 servings*

*2 pounds firm-fleshed fish, such as sea
    bass or snapper*
½ cup chicken-flavor bouillon or stock
¼ cup dry sherry
1 tablespoon soy sauce

½ teaspoon grated fresh gingerroot
2 teaspoons cornstarch
1 tablespoon water
1 packet Sweet 'N Low
1 tablespoon Dijon mustard

Preheat broiler. Spray rack over broiler pan with nonstick coating agent. Wipe fish with paper towel and place on broiler rack. In small saucepan, combine bouillon, sherry, soy sauce, and ginger; bring to simmering over moderate heat. Combine cornstarch with water and add to sauce. Stir until mixture thickens; remove from heat. Stir in Sweet 'N Low. Brush fish with ¼ cup sauce. Broil 6 to 8 minutes, brushing fish twice with sauce. Fish is cooked when it flakes easily with a fork. Mix mustard with remaining sauce and serve over fish.

PER SERVING (5 ounces):		Calories: 163		Cholesterol: 62mg
Protein: 28gm	Carbohydrate: 3gm		Fat: 3gm	Sodium: 415mg

Sweet 'N Sour Shrimp   *4 servings*

¼ cup thinly sliced onion
*1 medium-size green pepper, seeded and
    cut into strips*
2 teaspoons vegetable oil
¼ cup rice vinegar
1 tablespoon soy sauce
2 teaspoons cornstarch

½ teaspoon ginger
*1 can (8 ounces) juice-packed crushed
    pineapple*
*1 pound shrimp, cooked, shelled, and
    deveined*
6 packets Sweet 'N Low

In large nonstick skillet or wok, sauté onion and green pepper in oil until onion is transparent. In separate bowl, mix together vinegar, soy sauce, cornstarch, and ginger. Stir in pineapple and add to skillet. Stir over low heat until mixture thickens. Stir in shrimp and Sweet 'N Low. Heat thoroughly. Serve over hot cooked rice.

PER SERVING (1¼ cups):		Calories: 175		Cholesterol: 140mg
Protein: 19gm	Carbohydrate: 15gm		Fat: 4gm	Sodium: 400mg

Bulgur-Stuffed Salmon Steaks (page 32)

Crab and Cheese Casserole   *6 servings*

2 tablespoons vegetable oil
1 cup sliced celery
½ cup sliced onion
½ cup thinly sliced carrot
½ cup sliced mushrooms
¼ cup diced green pepper
1 can (2 pounds) whole tomatoes

1½ cups fresh or frozen flaked
   crabmeat
1 cup cooked brown rice
¼ teaspoon salt
1 packet Sweet 'N Low
1 bay leaf
½ cup (2 ounces) grated sharp Cheddar
   cheese

Preheat oven to 350°F. Heat oil in Dutch oven or other ovenproof container. Sauté celery, onion, carrot, mushrooms, and green pepper until onion is transparent. Add remaining ingredients, except cheese. Let simmer 5 minutes. Remove bay leaf. Sprinkle with cheese. Bake 20 minutes.

PER SERVING (1¼ cups):   Calories: 202   Cholesterol: 49mg
Protein: 13gm   Carbohydrate: 18gm   Fat: 9gm   Sodium: 526mg

Bulgur-Stuffed Salmon Steaks   *8 servings*

1 cup bulgur
2 envelopes low-sodium instant chicken
   broth and seasoning mix
2 cups hot water
⅓ cup minced parsley
⅓ cup minced scallions
1 clove garlic, minced
3 teaspoons dried dill, divided
½ teaspoon celery seed

½ teaspoon Nu-Salt *salt substitute*
⅛ teaspoon freshly ground pepper
2 tablespoons liquid Butter Buds
2 tablespoons white wine
1 tablespoon lemon juice
2 pounds fresh or frozen, thawed salmon
   steaks, cut 1 inch thick
Alfalfa sprouts
Lemon wedges

Preheat oven to 375°F. In medium-size bowl, combine bulgur, broth mix, and water; let stand 30 minutes. Add parsley, scallions, garlic, 2 teaspoons dill, celery seed, Nu-Salt, and pepper; set aside. In cup, stir together Butter Buds, white wine, lemon juice, and remaining 1 teaspoon dill; set aside. Spoon half of bulgur mixture into 10-inch-square casserole. Place salmon steaks on top of bulgur. Spoon remaining bulgur mixture into center cavity of each fish steak. Brush fish with Butter Buds mixture. Cover casserole loosely with aluminum foil. Bake 15 to 20 minutes or until fish flakes easily with fork. Serve with lemon wedges and alfalfa sprouts. (See photo, page 31.)

PER SERVING (3 ounces salmon and ½ cup bulgur):
                    Calories: 210   Cholesterol: 64mg
Protein: 19gm   Carbohydrate: 19gm   Fat: 6gm   Sodium: 85mg

Vegetables

Sautéed Potatoes *4 servings*

1 chicken-flavor bouillon cube
1 cup water
¼ cup liquid Butter Buds
¼ teaspoon garlic powder

¼ teaspoon basil
1 teaspoon parsley flakes
2 medium-size (8 to 10 ounces) baking
  potatoes

Combine bouillon and water in medium-size saucepan. Heat, stirring constantly, until bouillon dissolves. Add Butter Buds, garlic powder, basil, and parsley. Remove from heat, but keep warm. Peel potatoes and cut into ¼-inch thick slices. Boil in lightly salted water until tender, about 15 minutes. Drain. Add potatoes to sauce and mix gently to coat.

PER SERVING (½ cup):   Calories: 85   Cholesterol: trace
Protein: 2gm   Carbohydrate: 19gm   Fat: trace   Sodium: 367mg

By using Butter Buds instead of butter in this recipe, you have saved 94 calories and 35 mg cholesterol per serving.

Red Cabbage with Apples *6 servings*

6 cups coarsely shredded red cabbage
2½ cups (2 medium) peeled, sliced
  apples
¼ cup raisins
3 tablespoons red wine vinegar

1 tablespoon Butter Buds *Sprinkles*
2 teaspoons caraway seeds
¼ teaspoon Nu-Salt *salt substitute*
¼ teaspoon Sweet 'N Low

Preheat oven to 400°F. In large bowl, stir together all ingredients. Spoon into 10-inch pie plate. Bake 10 to 12 minutes. (See photo, page 35.)

PER SERVING (approximately 1 cup):   Calories: 70   Cholesterol: 0mg
Protein: 1gm   Carbohydrate: 17gm   Fat: 0gm   Sodium: 42mg

Corn on the Cob in the Husk   *4 servings*

4 ears unhusked corn   *¹/₄ teaspoon garlic salt*
1 packet Butter Buds, *made into liquid*

Peel down husks, do not detach, remove silk. Combine Butter Buds and garlic salt. Brush evenly over each ear of corn. Recover with husk. Heat 3 or 4 inches from coals or grill 20 to 30 minutes. Turn one-quarter the way around every 5 minutes. Remove husk and brush again with Butter Buds sauce. Serve remaining sauce with corn. (See photo, page 37.)

PER SERVING (1 ear of corn):		Calories: 90	Cholesterol: trace
Protein: 3gm	Carbohydrate: 19gm	Fat: 1gm	Sodium: 297mg

By using Butter Buds instead of butter in this recipe, you have saved 125 calories and 70 mg cholesterol per serving.

Stuffed Baked Potatoes   *2 servings*

3 medium-size (about 1 pound) baking   *¹/₄ teaspoon marjoram*
*   potatoes*   *Freshly ground pepper to taste*
³/₄ cup low fat milk   *3 tablespoons liquid* Butter Buds
1 packet Butter Buds   *Paprika*
1 slice reduced fat cheese food

Preheat oven to 400°F. Scrub potatoes and pierce several times with fork. Bake until tender, about 1 hour. Cut 1 potato in half and scoop out insides into bowl, discarding skin. Cut a thin slice off the tops of remaining potatoes and carefully scoop out insides, leaving about ½ inch of potato around inside of skin. Add scooped-out pulp to bowl with other potato pulp; reserve potato shells. Preheat broiler. Heat milk in top of double boiler. Add Butter Buds and stir until dissolved. Add cheese and marjoram, stirring constantly until cheese melts. Add hot liquid to potatoes. Beat until potatoes are light and free of lumps. (Add more milk if needed or desired for softer potatoes.) Add pepper. Spoon into potato shells, rounding tops. Brush tops with liquid Butter Buds and sprinkle with paprika. Broil until lightly browned. (See photo, page 37.)

PER SERVING (1 potato):		Calories: 264	Cholesterol: 13mg
Protein: 11gm	Carbohydrate: 46gm	Fat: 3gm	Sodium: 733mg

By using Butter Buds instead of butter in this recipe, you have saved 517 calories and 197 mg cholesterol per serving.

Red Cabbage with Apples (page 33)

Broccoli Cheese Pie   *6 servings*

*1 package (10 ounces) frozen chopped
  broccoli*
⅓ cup chopped onion
1 tablespoon lemon juice
½ teaspoon nutmeg
⅛ teaspoon freshly ground pepper

*9-inch Low-Sodium Pie Crust
  (page 57)*
⅓ cup grated Parmesan cheese
4 eggs
½ cup low fat milk
¼ cup liquid Butter Buds

Preheat oven to 425°F. Cook broccoli according to package directions; drain well. While broccoli is draining, combine onion, lemon juice, nutmeg, and pepper in medium-size bowl. Add broccoli and mix well. Pour into pie shell and sprinkle with Parmesan cheese. Mix eggs with milk and Butter Buds. Pour over broccoli mixture. Place filled pie pan on cookie sheet and bake 10 minutes. Reduce heat to 350°F and bake about 30 minutes, or until filling is set. (See photo, page 55.)

PER SERVING (⅙ pie):   Calories: 230   Cholesterol: 147mg
Protein: 11gm   Carbohydrate: 21gm   Fat: 11gm   Sodium: 335mg

Baked Sweet 'N Sour
Brussels Sprouts   *4 servings*

*1 package (10 ounces) frozen Brussels
  sprouts*
⅓ cup liquid Butter Buds, *divided*
2 tablespoons cider vinegar
1½ teaspoons sugar

¼ teaspoon tarragon
⅛ teaspoon marjoram
⅛ teaspoon freshly ground pepper
⅓ cup sliced fresh mushrooms
1 tablespoon chopped pimiento

Preheat oven to 350°F. Cook Brussels sprouts in small amount of unsalted water just until thawed. Drain. Arrange sprouts in shallow baking dish. Combine 4 table-spoons Butter Buds, vinegar, sugar, tarragon, marjoram, and pepper in blender container. Cover and process on medium speed a few seconds. Pour over sprouts. Combine remaining Butter Buds, mushrooms, and pimiento. Sprinkle over sprouts. Bake, covered, about 15 minutes, or until sprouts are tender.

PER SERVING (⅔ cup):   Calories: 47   Cholesterol: trace
Protein: 3gm   Carbohydrate: 9gm   Fat: trace   Sodium: 120mg

You can substitute ½ packet Sweet 'N Low for the sugar in this recipe. You'll save 5 calories and 1 gm carbohydrate per serving.

*Corn on the Cob in the Husk (page 34), Baked Sweet 'N Sour
Brussels Sprouts, Stuffed Baked Potatoes (page 34)*

Pasta

Rotelle with Pesto and Pimiento   *6 servings*

2 cups Italian parsley
½ cup grated Parmesan cheese
¼ cup pine nuts (pignoli)
2 cloves garlic, minced
2 tablespoons dried basil
¾ teaspoon Nu-Salt *salt substitute*

1 cup liquid Butter Buds
1 jar (4 ounces) sliced pimientos,
   drained
1 pound rotelle
2 tablespoons olive oil

In blender or food processor, blend parsley, cheese, pine nuts, garlic, basil, and Nu-Salt. Add Butter Buds and blend again. Transfer to large bowl and fold in pimientos. Cook pasta according to package directions but without salt; drain well. Add to sauce. Add oil; toss well.

PER SERVING (1¼ cups):		Calories: 255	Cholesterol: 7mg
Protein: 10gm	Carbohydrate: 32gm	Fat: 11gm	Sodium: 395mg

Poppy Seed Noodles   *4 servings*

6 ounces uncooked enriched egg noodles
2 packets Butter Buds, *made into liquid*
2 tablespoons minced onion

2½ teaspoons poppy seeds
¼ teaspoon onion powder

Prepare noodles according to package directions, omitting salt; drain. Combine ½ cup Butter Buds and onion in small saucepan. Cook over medium heat about 3 minutes, or just until onion is soft. Add cooked noodles, remaining Butter Buds, poppy seeds, and onion powder. Heat thoroughly.

PER SERVING (¾ cup):		Calories: 201	Cholesterol: 42mg
Protein: 6gm	Carbohydrate: 36gm	Fat: 3gm	Sodium: 344mg

By using Butter Buds instead of butter in this recipe, you have saved 376 calories and 140 mg cholesterol per serving.

Rotelle with Pesto and Pimiento

Spinach Noodle Fettucine   *4 servings*

1 cup low fat cottage cheese
½ cup plain low fat yogurt
½ cup thinly sliced water chestnuts
½ cup toasted slivered almonds, divided
¼ cup finely chopped pimiento
1 packet Butter Buds
1 tablespoon chopped fresh parsley

1 tablespoon grated Parmesan cheese
¼ teaspoon oregano
¼ teaspoon basil
¼ teaspoon thyme
Freshly ground pepper to taste
8 ounces (4 cups) uncooked spinach
 noodles

In medium-size bowl, blend cottage cheese into yogurt. Add remaining ingredients except noodles, using only ⅓ cup almonds. Mix well. Prepare noodles according to package directions, omitting salt. Drain. In a warm pan, toss with cheese mixture. Turn onto warm serving platter and sprinkle with remaining almonds.

| PER SERVING (1¼ cups): | | Calories: 416 | Cholesterol: 59mg |
| Protein: 21gm | Carbohydrate: 54gm | Fat: 13gm | Sodium: 453mg |

By using Butter Buds instead of butter in this recipe, you have saved 188 calories and 70 mg cholesterol per serving.

Noodle Pudding   *4 servings*

2 ounces uncooked enriched noodles
2 eggs
1 cup evaporated skim milk, undiluted
½ cup part skim ricotta cheese
3 packets Sweet 'N Low

1 teaspoon vanilla
1 teaspoon grated lemon peel
1 medium-size apple, peeled and grated
¼ cup raisins

Preheat oven to 350°F. Cook noodles according to package directions, omitting salt. With electric mixer, beat eggs in large bowl. Add milk, ricotta cheese, Sweet 'N Low, vanilla, and lemon peel. Beat until smooth. Stir in noodles, apple, and raisins. Turn into 1-quart casserole. Bake 1 hour, or until knife inserted in center comes out clean.

| PER SERVING (½ cup): | | Calories: 237 | Cholesterol: 132mg |
| Protein: 14gm | Carbohydrate: 32gm | Fat: 6gm | Sodium: 148mg |

Sauces and Dressings

Herb Salad Dressing *About ⅔ cup*

1 packet Butter Buds, *made into liquid*
1 tablespoon distilled white vinegar
1 tablespoon lemon juice
¼ teaspoon garlic powder

¼ teaspoon oregano
¼ teaspoon tarragon
¼ teaspoon thyme
⅛ teaspoon freshly ground pepper

Combine all ingredients in small jar; cover and shake until well blended. Serve over your favorite tossed green salad. (See photo, page 13.)

PER SERVING (1 tablespoon): Calories: 6 Cholesterol: trace
Protein: trace Carbohydrate: 1gm Fat: trace Sodium: 69mg

Herb Butter Sauce *½ cup*

1 packet Butter Buds, *made into liquid*
2 tablespoons lemon juice
1 teaspoon parsley flakes

1 teaspoon dehydrated chives
½ teaspoon tarragon
⅛ teaspoon onion powder

Combine all ingredients in small saucepan and heat just until' hot, mixing well. Spoon sauce over your favorite vegetable or meat crêpe.

PER SERVING (1 tablespoon): Calories: 7 Cholesterol: trace
Protein: trace Carbohydrate: 1gm Fat: trace Sodium: 86mg

By using Butter Buds instead of butter in this recipe, you have saved 188 calories and 70 mg cholesterol per serving.

Breads and Crêpes

Banana Toast *4 servings*

1 packet Butter Buds, *mixed with ¼ cup*
  hot water
1 tablespoon honey

¼ teaspoon cinnamon
4 slices enriched white toast
2 medium-size bananas, thinly sliced

Preheat broiler. In covered jar, combine Butter Buds, honey, and cinnamon; shake well. With pastry brush, spread sauce on each slice of toast. Arrange banana slices on toast, covering entire surface. Brush with additional sauce. Broil 2 to 3 minutes, or until bananas begin to bubble.

PER SERVING (1 slice):		Calories: 147		Cholesterol: 2mg
Protein: 3gm	Carbohydrate: 32gm		Fat: 1gm	Sodium: 295mg

By using Butter Buds instead of butter in this recipe, you have saved 188 calories and 70 mg cholesterol per serving.

Bran Muffins *2 dozen muffins*

4 cups raisin bran cereal
2½ cups all-purpose flour
1½ cups sugar
2½ teaspoons baking soda

1 teaspoon salt
2 eggs
2 cups buttermilk
1 packet Butter Buds, *made into liquid*

Preheat oven to 400°F. In large bowl, mix cereal, flour, sugar, baking soda, and salt. Add eggs, buttermilk, and Butter Buds and mix well. Spray muffin tins with nonstick coating agent. Fill muffin cups two-thirds full and bake 15 to 20 minutes.

PER SERVING (1 muffin):		Calories: 137		Cholesterol: 19mg
Protein: 3gm	Carbohydrate: 30gm		Fat: 1gm	Sodium: 293mg

By using Butter Buds instead of butter in this recipe, you have saved 31 calories and 12 mg cholesterol per serving.

Blueberry Muffins   *1 dozen muffins*

2¼ *cups all-purpose flour, divided*
½ *cup sugar*
1 *tablespoon baking powder*
½ *teaspoon salt*
¾ *cup low fat milk*

¼ *cup liquid* Butter Buds
1 *egg, lightly beaten*
1½ *cups fresh or frozen, thawed*
   blueberries

Preheat oven to 400°F. In large bowl, combine 2 cups of the flour, sugar, baking powder, and salt. Stir in milk, Butter Buds, and egg until just moistened. Rinse and drain blueberries; toss with remaining ¼ cup flour. Gently fold blueberries into batter. Spoon equally into twelve 2½-inch muffin pan cups sprayed with nonstick coating agent. Bake 20 to 25 minutes or until golden brown. Remove from pan and cool on wire rack.

PER SERVING (1 muffin):		Calories: 143	Cholesterol: 18mg
Protein: 4gm	Carbohydrate: 30gm	Fat: 1gm	Sodium: 240mg

By using Butter Buds instead of butter in this recipe, you have saved 27 calories and 12 mg cholesterol per serving.

Cranberry Nut Loaf   *18 servings*

2½ *cups sifted all-purpose flour*
¾ *cup sugar*
½ *cup low fat milk*
1 *packet* Butter Buds, *made into liquid*
1 *egg*

3½ *teaspoons baking powder*
½ *teaspoon salt*
1 *cup coarsely chopped cranberries*
¼ *cup chopped walnuts*

Preheat oven to 350°F. In large bowl, combine flour, sugar, milk, Butter Buds, egg, baking powder, and salt. Beat with electric mixer on medium speed 30 seconds, or just until moistened, scraping sides and bottom of bowl. Stir in cranberries and walnuts. Turn batter into nonstick 9 × 5-inch loaf pan. Bake 55 to 65 minutes, or until toothpick inserted in center comes out clean. Remove from pan; cool thoroughly before slicing.

PER SERVING (one ½-inch slice):		Calories: 114	Cholesterol: 12mg
Protein: 3gm	Carbohydrate: 22gm	Fat: 2gm	Sodium: 189mg

By using Butter Buds instead of butter in this recipe, you have saved 42 calories and 16 mg cholesterol per serving.

Blueberry Muffins, Super Chocolate Chip Cookies (page 53),
Low-Sodium Brownies (page 57), Cranberry Nut Loaf

Baked Carrot Squares   *16 servings*

1 cup sifted all-purpose flour
1 teaspoon baking powder
¼ teaspoon cinnamon
⅛ teaspoon nutmeg
⅛ teaspoon salt
6 packets Sweet 'N Low

½ teaspoon baking soda
1 packet Butter Buds, *made into liquid*
1 egg, beaten
1 cup grated carrots
1 cup raisins

Preheat oven to 350°F. Spray 8-inch square baking pan with nonstick coating agent. In medium-size bowl, combine flour, baking powder, cinnamon, nutmeg, salt, and Sweet 'N Low. In separate bowl, dissolve baking soda in Butter Buds; add to dry ingredients. Stir in egg. Add carrots and raisins and mix thoroughly. Pour into prepared pan. Bake 30 minutes, or until toothpick inserted in center comes out clean. Cool and cut into 2-inch squares.

PER SERVING (one 2-inch square):   Calories: 66   Cholesterol: 13mg
Protein: 2gm   Carbohydrate: 14gm   Fat: trace   Sodium: 121mg

By using Butter Buds instead of butter in this recipe, you have saved 47 calories and 18 mg cholesterol per serving.

Applesauce Nut Bread   *18 servings*

1 cup sifted all-purpose flour
1 cup whole wheat flour
⅓ cup sugar
6 packets Sweet 'N Low
1 tablespoon baking powder
½ teaspoon salt

½ teaspoon nutmeg
½ teaspoon baking soda
1 cup chopped walnuts
1 egg
1 cup unsweetened applesauce
¼ cup vegetable oil

Preheat oven to 350°F. Spray 9 × 5-inch loaf pan with nonstick coating agent. In large bowl, sift together dry ingredients; stir in nuts. In separate bowl, beat egg with electric mixer until frothy, about 30 seconds. Stir in applesauce and oil. Add to dry ingredients and stir just until blended. Pour into prepared pan. Bake 1 hour, or until toothpick inserted in center comes out clean.

PER SERVING (one ½-inch slice):   Calories: 141   Cholesterol: 12mg
Protein: 3gm   Carbohydrate: 16gm   Fat: 8gm   Sodium: 160mg

By substituting ¼ cup liquid Butter Buds for the vegetable oil in this recipe, you can save 25 calories, 3 gm of fat, and 8 mg cholesterol. However, you will add 15 mg of sodium.

Asparagus Cheese Crêpes *4 servings*

---

*1 package (10 ounces) frozen cut
  asparagus*
1 cup low fat cottage cheese
2 tablespoons low fat milk

1 tablespoon fresh lemon juice
1½ teaspoons minced onion flakes
8 Low-Calorie Crêpes (below)
Herb Butter Sauce (page 42)

Preheat oven to 350°F. Cook asparagus according to package directions; drain well.
Chop into small pieces; place in medium-size bowl. In blender container, combine
cottage cheese, milk, lemon juice, and onion flakes. Cover and process at medium
speed 20 to 30 seconds. Fold cheese mixture into chopped asparagus. Fill crêpes
with 2 rounded tablespoons of cheese mixture. Fold over and place in nonstick baking dish. Bake, covered, 15 to 20 minutes, or until heated through. Before serving,
spoon about 1 tablespoon Herb Butter Sauce over each crêpe. (See photo, page 55.)

PER SERVING (2 crêpes):   Calories: 220   Cholesterol: 112mg
Protein: 17gm   Carbohydrate: 28gm   Fat: 4gm   Sodium: 628mg

---

Low-Calorie Crêpes *12 crêpes*

---

1 cup all-purpose flour
1¼ cups low fat milk
1 packet Butter Buds

3 eggs
⅛ teaspoon salt

Mixer or whisk method: In medium bowl, combine all ingredients. Beat with electric mixer or whisk until smooth.

Blender method: Combine ingredients in blender container. Cover and process at
medium speed about 1 minute. Scrape down sides with rubber spatula and blend for
another 15 seconds, or until smooth.

Refrigerate 1 hour or more. If batter separates, stir gently before cooking. Cook on
upside-down crêpe griddle or in traditional pan.

PER SERVING (1 crêpe):   Calories: 71   Cholesterol: 54mg
Protein: 3gm   Carbohydrate: 10gm   Fat: 1gm   Sodium: 109mg

---

*By using Butter Buds instead of butter in this recipe, you have saved 63 calories and
23 mg cholesterol per serving.*

Chinese Crêpes with Apricot Filling and Peanuts *8 servings*

Crêpes
1 large egg
¾ cup all-purpose flour
½ teaspoon Sweet 'N Low
¼ teaspoon Nu-Salt *salt substitute*
1 cup low fat milk
2 tablespoons margarine, melted
1 teaspoon vegetable oil

Filling
*2 cans (15 ounces each) unpeeled
apricot halves, packed in juice,
drained*

¾ cup water, divided
1 tablespoon liquid Butter Buds
2 tablespoons cornstarch

Topping
2 teaspoons vegetable oil
½ cup chopped raw unsalted peanuts
2 tablespoons sugar
½ teaspoon Sweet 'N Low

In medium-size bowl, combine egg, flour, ½ teaspoon Sweet 'N Low, and Nu-Salt. With wire whisk, stir in milk and melted margarine. Heat a well-seasoned crêpe pan or small nonstick skillet with rounded sides; add 1 teaspoon oil. With paper towel, spread oil to coat surface of pan. Add about ¼ cup of batter to cover bottom of pan. Cook briefly and turn. Cook briefly and turn out onto waxed paper. Repeat until all batter is used. Set crêpes aside.

Filling: Place apricot halves in small saucepan and add ½ cup water. Cook, stirring and mashing down to thicken the fruit, about 3 minutes. Add Butter Buds and continue cooking, stirring to make a paste, about 5 minutes. In cup, combine cornstarch and remaining ¼ cup water. Stir into apricots. Set filling aside.

Topping: In medium-size nonstick skillet, heat 2 teaspoons oil. Add peanuts and cook, stirring, just until golden. Do not overcook. Remove to paper towels and drain. Place peanuts in small bowl; add sugar and ½ teaspoon Sweet 'N Low. Set aside.

Preheat oven to 250°F. Spray cookie sheet with nonstick cooking spray. Place crêpes on cookie sheet. Spoon about ¼ cup of filling onto center of each crêpe and fold crêpe over, envelope-fashion. Bake about 10 minutes. Sprinkle each crêpe with 1 tablespoon peanut topping. Serve warm.

PER SERVING (1 crêpe):		Calories: 185		Cholesterol: 36mg
Protein: 5gm	Carbohydrate: 24gm		Fat: 8gm	Sodium: 40mg

Desserts

Cheesecake *8 servings*

2 envelopes unflavored gelatin
¼ cup sugar, divided
¼ teaspoon salt
2 packets Butter Buds, divided
½ cup plus 3 tablespoons unsweetened
  pineapple juice, divided
1 cup low fat milk
2 eggs, separated

1 container (8 ounces) dry curd cottage
  cheese
½ cup juice-packed crushed pineapple,
  drained
1 tablespoon grated lemon peel
½ cup graham cracker crumbs
1 teaspoon vanilla
1 tablespoon lemon juice

Mix gelatin, 3 tablespoons sugar, salt, 1 packet Butter Buds, ½ cup pineapple juice, milk, and egg yolks in top of double boiler. Place over boiling water and cook, stirring constantly, until gelatin dissolves and mixture thickens slightly. Cool. In medium-size bowl, beat cottage cheese until smooth. (Use a potato masher for best results.) Beat in crushed pineapple and lemon peel. Add cooled gelatin mixture. In separate small bowl, combine graham cracker crumbs, remaining packet Butter Buds, and vanilla. Add remaining pineapple juice and lemon juice. Mix well. Stir into cheese mixture. In separate bowl, beat egg whites until they hold their shape. Gradually add remaining sugar and beat until stiff. Fold into cheese-crumb mixture. Pour into 9-inch pie plate. Chill until firm.

PER SERVING (⅛ of cake):		Calories: 152		Cholesterol: 57mg
Protein: 10gm	Carbohydrate: 22gm		Fat: 2gm	Sodium: 320mg

By using Butter Buds instead of butter in this recipe, you have saved 188 calories and 70 mg cholesterol per serving. You can also substitute 6 packets Sweet 'N Low for the sugar in this recipe and save 20 calories and 5 gm carbohydrates per serving.

*Chocolate Mousse (page 52), Cheesecake,
Cherry Dumplings (page 52)*

Chocolate Mousse   *8 servings*

1 envelope unflavored gelatin
2 tablespoons unsweetened cocoa
2 eggs, separated
2 cups evaporated skim milk, divided

¼ cup sugar
2 packets Sweet 'N Low
1½ teaspoons vanilla

In medium-size saucepan, mix gelatin and cocoa. In separate bowl, beat egg yolks with 1 cup milk. Blend into gelatin mixture. Let stand 1 minute to soften gelatin. Stir over low heat until gelatin is completely dissolved, about 5 minutes. Add remaining milk, sugar, Sweet 'N Low, and vanilla. Pour into large bowl and chill, stirring occasionally, until mixture mounds slightly when dropped from spoon. In separate large bowl, beat egg whites until soft peaks form; gradually add gelatin mixture and beat until doubled in volume, about 5 minutes. Chill until mixture is slightly thickened. Turn into dessert dishes or 1-quart bowl and chill until set. (See photo, page 51.)

PER SERVING (½ cup):   Calories: 103   Cholesterol: 56mg
Protein: 7gm   Carbohydrate: 15gm   Fat: 2gm   Sodium: 91mg

Cherry Dumplings   *4 servings*

1 can (1 pound) pitted, water-packed
   tart red cherries, undrained
3 tablespoons sugar
1 packet Butter Buds
¾ teaspoon cornstarch

¾ cup sifted cake flour
¾ teaspoon baking powder
⅛ teaspoon salt
1 tablespoon grated orange peel
1 tablespoon low fat milk

Preheat oven to 350°F. In saucepan, combine cherries with juice, sugar, Butter Buds, and cornstarch. Bring to a boil. Remove from heat and transfer to 1-quart baking dish. In small bowl, mix flour, baking powder, and salt. Add orange peel, milk, and 3 tablespoons hot cherry sauce. Mix lightly until moist. Drop tablespoonfuls into cherry sauce to make 4 dumplings. Cover and bake about 20 minutes, or until dumplings become light and cherries bubble. Serve warm. (See photo, page 51.)

PER SERVING (1 dumpling with sauce):   Calories: 160   Cholesterol: trace
Protein: 2gm   Carbohydrate: 37gm   Fat: trace   Sodium: 330mg

By using Butter Buds instead of butter in this recipe, you have saved 188 calories and 70 mg cholesterol per serving. You can also substitute 4 packets Sweet 'N Low for the sugar in this recipe and save 30 calories and 8 gm carbohydrates per serving.

Super Chocolate Chip Cookies *About 4 dozen cookies*

1 packet Butter Buds, *made into liquid*
¼ cup vegetable oil
1 cup sugar
2 eggs
1 teaspoon vanilla
1 cup sifted all-purpose flour

1 cup sifted whole wheat flour
1 teaspoon baking soda
½ teaspoon salt
1 package (6 ounces) chocolate chips
2 cups 40% bran flakes cereal

Preheat oven to 425°F. Spray 2 cookie sheets with nonstick coating agent. In large mixing bowl, combine Butter Buds, oil, and sugar. Beat in eggs and vanilla. Mix dry ingredients; add to creamed mixture. Stir in chocolate chips and cereal. Drop by rounded teaspoonfuls onto prepared cookie sheets. Bake 8 to 10 minutes. Remove cookies immediately to cooling racks. (See photo, page 45.)

PER SERVING (1 cookie):		Calories: 71		Cholesterol: 10mg
Protein: 1gm	Carbohydrate: 11gm		Fat: 3gm	Sodium: 75mg

By using Butter Buds instead of butter in this recipe, you have saved 16 calories and 6 mg cholesterol per cookie.

Almond Cookies *2½ dozen cookies*

1 cup sifted all-purpose flour
½ teaspoon baking powder
⅛ teaspoon salt
¼ cup vegetable shortening or margarine

1 packet Butter Buds
¼ cup plus 2 tablespoons sugar
1 egg
2 teaspoons almond extract
3 tablespoons sliced almonds

Preheat oven to 350°F. Sift together flour, baking powder, and salt. Cut in shortening. Stir in Butter Buds, sugar, egg, and almond extract to make a soft dough. Add a small amount of water if needed. Refrigerate for 15 minutes. Form into one-inch balls. Press an almond slice into the center of each ball. Arrange 2 inches apart on a nonstick cookie sheet. Bake 5 minutes, then flatten cookies with spatula to ¼-inch thickness. Continue baking 8 to 10 minutes longer, or until lightly browned.

PER SERVING (1 cookie):		Calories: 47		Cholesterol: 7mg
Protein: trace	Carbohydrate: 6gm		Fat: 2gm	Sodium: 41mg

By using Butter Buds instead of butter in this recipe, you have saved 25 calories and 9 mg cholesterol per cookie.

Bran-Apple Cookies

1²/₃ cups sifted all-purpose flour	½ cup diet margarine
1 teaspoon baking soda	6 packets Sweet 'N Low
¼ teaspoon nutmeg	1 egg
¼ teaspoon ground cloves	1 cup unsweetened applesauce
¼ teaspoon allspice	⅓ cup golden raisins
¼ teaspoon salt	1 cup 40% bran flakes cereal

Preheat oven to 375°F. Sift dry ingredients into medium-size bowl. In separate bowl, beat margarine, Sweet 'N Low, and egg until light and fluffy. Alternately add dry ingredients and applesauce, mixing well after each addition. Stir in raisins and cereal. Drop by rounded teaspoons onto nonstick cookie sheets. Bake 15 minutes, or until golden brown.

PER SERVING (1 cookie):   Calories: 44   Cholesterol: 6mg
Protein: trace   Carbohydrate: 7gm   Fat: 1gm   Sodium: 81mg

Poached Pears
with Blueberry Sauce

8 medium-size (about 2½ pounds) fresh pears	4 packets Sweet 'N Low
1 packet Butter Buds	2 cups fresh or frozen unsweetened blueberries
1 cup water	¼ cup port wine
3 tablespoons lemon juice	

Preheat oven to 350°F. Peel pears, leaving stems intact; do not core. Arrange with stems up in 3-quart casserole; set aside. Combine Butter Buds, water, lemon juice, and Sweet 'N Low; mix well. Pour over pears. Bake, covered, 45 minutes, or until pears are tender. Drain and chill, about 45 minutes. In blender container, process blueberries and wine, covered, on low several seconds, or until well blended. Place pears in shallow dish and pour blueberry sauce over top. Refrigerate, turning pears occasionally to coat well. Serve in dessert dishes topped with plain low fat yogurt, if desired.

PER SERVING (1 pear):   Calories: 113   Cholesterol: trace
Protein: trace   Carbohydrate: 26gm   Fat: trace   Sodium: 45mg

By using Butter Buds instead of butter in this recipe, you have saved 94 calories and 35 mg cholesterol per serving.

Asparagus Cheese Crêpes (page 47), Poached Pears with Blueberry Sauce, Broccoli Cheese Pie (page 36)

Easy Sticky Buns *8 servings*

1 packet Butter Buds, *made into liquid*
¼ cup chopped nuts
¼ cup flaked coconut
3 tablespoons firmly packed light brown
  sugar

1 teaspoon cinnamon
1 package (10½ ounces) refrigerated
  biscuits

Preheat oven to 350°F. In round cake pan or baking dish, combine all ingredients except biscuits. Separate biscuits and roll in syrup mixture to coat. Arrange in single layer on top of syrup. Bake 15 to 20 minutes, or until buns are well browned. While still warm, invert on serving plate.

PER SERVING (1 bun):   Calories: 164   Cholesterol: trace
Protein: 3gm   Carbohydrate: 25gm   Fat: 5gm   Sodium: 416mg

By using Butter Buds instead of butter in this recipe, you have saved 94 calories and 35 mg cholesterol per serving.

Lemon Chiffon Pie *12 servings*

1½ cups graham cracker or gingersnap
  crumbs
⅓ cup margarine, melted
3 tablespoons sugar
1 envelope unflavored gelatin
1 tablespoon grated lemon peel

3 packets Sweet 'N Low
⅛ teaspoon salt
4 eggs, separated
½ cup water
⅓ cup fresh lemon juice

Preheat oven to 375°F. Combine cracker crumbs and margarine; press into bottom and up sides of 9-inch pie plate. Bake 6 to 8 minutes. Cool on wire rack.

In small saucepan, combine sugar, gelatin, lemon peel, Sweet 'N Low, and salt. Lightly beat egg yolks with water and lemon juice; gradually stir into gelatin mixture. Cook over low heat, stirring constantly, until slightly thickened, about 10 minutes. Pour into a large bowl. Cover and chill until mixture mounds slightly when dropped from a spoon, about 1½ hours. Beat egg whites until stiff peaks form. Gently fold into lemon mixture. Pour into pie crust. Cover and chill until firm, about 5 hours. Garnish top with additional grated lemon peel, if desired.

PER SERVING (1/12 of pie):   Calories: 147   Cholesterol: 71mg
Protein: 4gm   Carbohydrate: 15gm   Fat: 8gm   Sodium: 194mg

Low-Sodium Pie Crust   *8 servings*

1 cup sifted all-purpose flour
1 packet Butter Buds
¼ teaspoon cinnamon
⅛ teaspoon mace

1 teaspoon sesame seeds
2 tablespoons plus 1 teaspoon
vegetable oil
2 to 3 tablespoons ice water

Blend flour with Butter Buds, cinnamon, mace, and sesame seeds. Add oil gradually, mixing into flour with a fork. When all of the oil has been added, work mixture lightly between fingertips until mixture is the size of small peas. Gradually add just enough ice water until dough is moist enough to hold together. Do not overwork dough. Form into a ball and roll out on floured surface with floured rolling pin, to a circle 1 inch larger than inverted 8- or 9-inch pie pan. Carefully transfer pastry to pie plate. Press dough into bottom and sides of pan, gently patting out air pockets. Preheat oven to 450°F. Prick bottom and sides of pastry with fork. Bake 8 to 10 minutes, or until lightly golden brown. Cool before using.

PER SERVING (⅛ of crust):   Calories: 96   Cholesterol: trace
Protein: 2gm   Carbohydrate: 12gm   Fat: 4gm   Sodium: 86mg

By using Butter Buds instead of butter in this recipe, you have saved 94 calories and 35 mg cholesterol per serving.

Low-Sodium Brownies   *16 brownies*

2 eggs, separated
¼ cup plus 1 tablespoon granulated
sugar, divided
½ cup firmly packed light brown sugar
1 teaspoon vanilla

½ cup unsweetened cocoa
½ cup liquid Butter Buds
½ cup sifted all-purpose flour
½ cup chopped walnuts

Preheat oven to 325°F. Beat yolks until light and lemon colored. Add ¼ cup granulated sugar and brown sugar and cream until light and fluffy. Blend in vanilla, cocoa, and Butter Buds. Add flour and mix thoroughly. Stir in chopped nuts. In separate bowl, beat egg whites until firm. Add 1 tablespoon granulated sugar and beat until stiff. Fold beaten whites into batter. When completely blended, transfer batter to nonstick 8-inch square baking dish. Bake 15 minutes, or until toothpick inserted in center comes out clean. (See photo, page 45.)

PER SERVING (1 brownie):   Calories: 98   Cholesterol: 27mg
Protein: 2gm   Carbohydrate: 16gm   Fat: 4gm   Sodium: 53mg

By using Butter Buds instead of butter in this recipe, you have saved 47 calories and 18 mg cholesterol per brownie.

Beverages

Glogg *16 servings*

5 whole cloves
1 cinnamon stick
½ teaspoon ground cardamom
½ teaspoon ground ginger
½ teaspoon ground nutmeg

½ gallon dry red wine
¼ cup plus 2 tablespoons sugar
1½ teaspoons Sweet 'N Low
1 cup blanched almond slivers
1 cup raisins

In large pot, combine spices and wine. Let stand overnight. Stir in sugar and Sweet 'N Low. Over medium heat, heat almost to a boil. Remove from heat; stir in almonds and raisins. Serve hot.

PER SERVING (½ cup):	Calories: 170	Cholesterol: 0mg
Protein: 2gm	Carbohydrate: 16gm Fat: 4gm	Sodium: 10mg

Spicy Iced Tea *4 cups*

4 tea bags
½ lemon, cut into slices
2 packets Sweet 'N Low

3 cinnamon sticks
8 whole cloves
4 cups boiling water

Combine tea bags, lemon, Sweet 'N Low, cinnamon, and cloves in a heat-proof pitcher. Pour in water. Let stand 1 hour, until cooled. Remove tea bags. Chill tea in refrigerator. Strain before serving.

PER SERVING (1 cup): Calories and nutrients insignificant.

Index